First Facts®

Expert Pet Care

CARING
for
Fish

A 4D BOOK

by Tammy Gagne

Consultant:
Jennifer Zablotny, DVM
Member, American Veterinary Medical Association

PEBBLE
a capstone imprint

Download the Capstone app!

- Ask an adult to download the Capstone 4D app.
- Scan the cover and stars inside the book for additional content.

When you scan a spread, you'll find fun extra stuff to go with this book! You can also find these things on the web at www.capstone4D.com using the password: fishcare.27414

First Facts are published by Pebble
1710 Roe Crest Drive, North Mankato, Minnesota 56003
www.mycapstone.com

Library of Congress Cataloging-in-Publication Data
is available on the Library of Congress website.

ISBN 978-1-5435-2741-4 (library binding)
ISBN 978-1-5435-2747-6 (paperback)
ISBN 978-1-5435-2753-7 (ebook pdf)

Editorial Credits
Marissa Kirkman, editor; Sarah Bennett, designer; Tracy Cummins, media researcher; Laura Manthe, production specialist

Photo Credits
Alamy: Juniors Bildarchiv GmbH, 9; Capstone Studio: Karon Dubke, 5, 7, 13, 16; iStockphoto: tc397, 18; Shutterstock: anusorn2005, Cover, bluehand, 3, Chaikom, 7 Inset, chonlasub woravichan, 21 Top, Cultura Motion, 8, ekmelica, Design Element, julie deshaies, 23, Kateryna Dyellalova, 21 Middle Right, Mike Richter, 20, Mirko Rosenau, 11, Napat, Back Cover, 24, PAUL ATKINSON, 21 Middle Left, Pavel Pomoleyko, 17, Podolnaya Elena, 21 Bottom, Steve Bower, 15, UMA SEN, 10, Vojce, 4, 19; SuperStock: NHPA, 12.

Printed in the United States of America.
PA017

Table of Contents

Your New Pet Fish

Many people enjoy watching colorful fish swim around in tanks. Fish make great pets. But you must learn a few things about them before setting up your own tank.

You can buy fish at pet stores. Ask someone at a store about which kinds of fish can live together peacefully.

FACT

Some fish live in freshwater. Others live in saltwater. Talk with your family about which type of fish will make the best pet for you.

These colorful fish live in saltwater.

Supplies You Will Need

You will need to set up an **aquarium** for your fish before bringing them home. Every fish tank needs a heater and a **filter**. These items keep the water warm and clean. You will need gravel for the bottom of the tank.

You will also need food for your fish. You can buy supplies and a small net at your pet supply store. You will need the net to safely move your fish in and out of the tank.

aquarium—a glass tank where pets, including hamsters, hermit crabs, and fish, are kept

filter—a tool that cleans water as it passes through it

oxygen—a colorless gas that people and animals breathe; humans and animals need oxygen to live

Some fish also need air stones.
They help fish breathe better
by adding **oxygen** to the water.

Bringing Your Fish Home

Pet stores place fish in plastic bags with water. Float your fish inside of these plastic bags in your aquarium. This helps the fish get used to the water **temperature** in the tank. Use a small net to move the fish. Do not mix the store's water into your tank.

Protect your fish from other pets. Cats may try to hunt fish. Some fish will also fight with other fish.

FACT

Your fish may lose some of their color on the way home. Their normal color will return as they adjust to their new home.

temperature—the measure of how hot or cold something is

Feeding Your Fish

Fish food looks like small flakes. Sprinkle the food into the water twice daily. How much food depends on the number and size of your fish. Watch the clock. It should take your fish about five minutes to eat.

Feeding too much or too little food can make your fish sick. Giving just the right amount of food and sticking to a **schedule** are important.

FACT

Some types of fish eat frozen food such as **krill**. Other fish eat live food called brine shrimp.

brine shrimp

schedule—a plan telling when things will happen

10 **krill**—a small, shrimp-like animal

Cleaning Your Aquarium

Clean your aquarium every two weeks. Use a sponge to keep the glass clean. Never use soap because it will kill your fish. You can use a **siphon** hose to clean the bottom of the tank.

Add clean water when you are done. It should be the same temperature as the rest.

FACT

You can safely remove one-third of the water during cleaning. This leaves enough water for your fish to stay in the tank while you clean it.

siphon

12 **siphon**—a tube that draws water upward

Keeping Your Fish Healthy

Watch your fish for signs that they are sick. Sick fish may stop eating, move slowly, or get white spots.

You can treat the tank water with medicine. Workers at the pet store can help you decide which type you need. Follow the directions carefully. Too much medicine can also hurt your pets.

Most **veterinarians** do not treat fish. Workers at the pet store may help you find a vet who does.

veterinarian—a doctor trained to take care of animals

Life with a Fish

Place the tank away from windows and direct sunlight. Fish need times of both light and darkness. Turn off the tank light each night. Turn it back on each morning.

Add some **decorations** to your tank. Plants, castles, or small ships make a tank look interesting. They also provide fish with spaces to swim through or hide in.

FACT

Large fish can be strong swimmers. A hood can keep them from jumping out of the tank.

decoration—a pretty, shiny, or colorful thing that is used to make some thing or place look nice

Your Fish Through the Years

Some types of fish live much longer than others. Some fish may only live two years. Others can live up to 20.

Make sure your tank is big enough for all the fish you add to it. Some fish can grow very large over time. You can keep your fish happy by making sure they have food and a clean tank.

FACT

An adult fish needs a tank about seven to 12 times its own length.

19

Fish Body Language

You can tell a lot about a fish by how it moves. Sick fish often swim on their sides. Scared fish will hide behind plants and other objects in the tank. A fish will usually stay in one place when it sleeps. It may still move its fins though.

Types of Fish

Freshwater fish:

- Goldfish
- Gourami
- Tetra

Gourami

Tetra

Angelfish

Tang

Saltwater fish:

- Angelfish
- Clownfish
- Tang

Glossary

aquarium (uh-KWAYR-ee-uhm)—a glass tank where pets, including hamsters, hermit crabs, and fish, are kept

decoration (dek-uh-REY-shuhn)—a pretty, shiny, or colorful thing that is used to make some thing or place look nice

filter (FIL-tuhr)—a tool that cleans water as it passes through it

krill (KRIL)—a small, shrimp-like animal

oxygen (OK-suh-juhn)—a colorless gas that people and animals breathe; humans and animals need oxygen to live

schedule (SKEJ-ul)—a plan telling when things will happen

siphon (SYE-fuhn)—a tube that draws water upward

temperature (TEM-pur-uh-chur)—the measure of how hot or cold something is

veterinarian (vet-ur-uh-NER-ee-uhn)—a doctor trained to take care of animals

Read More

Gardeski, Christina Mia. *Pet Fish: Questions and Answers*. Pet Questions and Answers. North Mankato, Minn.: Capstone Press, 2017.

Meister, Cari. *Fish*. My First Pet. Minneapolis: Bullfrog Books, 2015.

Rau, Dana Meachen. *Kids Top 10 Pet Fish*. American Humane Association Top 10 Pets for Kids. Berkeley Heights, N.J.: Enslow Elementary, 2015.

Internet Sites

Use FactHound to find
Internet sites related to this book.

Visit *www.facthound.com*

Just type in 9781543527414 and go.

Super-cool stuff!

Check out projects, games and lots more at
www.capstonekids.com

Critical Thinking Questions

1. Why do you need to float the plastic bag with your new fish inside of it at the top of the tank?

2. What are some of the ways in which you can keep the aquarium clean for your fish?

3. What should you do if your fish get sick?

Index